# *An* Incomplete Encyclopedia *of* Happiness *and* Unhappiness

ALSO BY AMY NEWMAN

*On this Day in Poetry History*
*Dear Editor*
*fall*
*Camera Lyrica*
*Order, or Disorder*

*An*
Incomplete
Encyclopedia
*of*
Happiness
*and*
Unhappiness

———

*Poems*

———

Amy
Newman

*A Karen & Michael Braziller Book*
Persea Books / New York

Persea Books, Inc.
90 Broad Street
New York, New York 10004

Library of Congress Cataloging-in-Publication Data

Names: Newman, Amy (Amy Lynn), author.
Title: An incomplete encyclopedia of happiness and unhappiness : poems / Amy Newman.
Description: First edition. | New York : Persea Books, [2023] | "A Karen & Michael Braziller book"
Identifiers: LCCN 2023022307 | ISBN 9780892556021 (paperback)
Subjects: LCGFT: Poetry.
Classification: LCC PS3564.E9148 I53 2023 | DDC 811/.54—dc23/eng/20230518
LC record available at https://lccn.loc.gov/2023022307

Book design and composition by Rita Lascaro
Typeset in Cardo.
Manufactured in the United States of America.
Printed on acid-free paper.

# Contents

_____

*for Joe*
*per tutto*

*for Billie Joe Armstrong*
*persistence rage eyeliner*

# INVOCATION

First, let us admit our imperfections.
And let us be forgiven our imperfections.
The saints to understand our imperfections.
  The human body formed of myth and air.

Let us cry the hurt of imperfections.
The landscape to mark the boundaries of these imperfections.
Let crushed shells escape the sea foam of the less perfect.
  The body a basket of sex and pretty violences.

How blessed are the castles of my imperfections!
To randomly number these imperfections:
Let birdsong distract the burden of imperfections.
  The human body formed of saint and ash.

Let a teacup hold as metaphor our imperfections.
Or that lake to be a poultice for our imperfections.
Flawless sky in ignorance of these imperfections.
  The body's troubles with gravity and air.

I try to wash the imperfections from me
But they stick like a dog on a red bone.
Who gives away this child of imperfection?
  I kiss the ring of My Imperfection.

Farmer of imperfection, your cows are out again!
Tie better the broken fence of your imperfections.
The trampled daisies imperfectly crushed.
  The sky awash in coming rains.

O house of imperfections with your cabinets of crusted honey!
I wash myself in a burden of want.
Let us bless the limbs in our tree of imperfections.
  The body a rebuttal of skin and hair.

# ABSOLUTION

Bless the imperfections. Forgive them.
Forgive the imperfection of the coming rain after four days of rain.
Forgive the imperfection of the aching shoulder blade.
Bless the childhood of indoor activity and books.
Forgive the escaped cow in the field with the daisies.

Bless the escaped cow and the broken stems of flower.
And the marriage counselor and the guidance counselor.
And the house that is rented and the shoreline disappearing.
Bless the contingent for its imperfections.
Forgive the cat who had to kill the mouse.

Bless the dog and the bone.
And the human who sings as an angel,
and the one who does not.
Forgive the small dead cat with the bite at her neck.
And whatever did the biting be forgiven.

Forgive the dying friend of his imperfections.
Bless his imperfections of blood and ruin.
Bless his perfect body as he will rise.
Forgive the long rehearsal and the orchard's loss.
Forgive the little imperfections and the large imperfections.

Bless the agents of real estate.
Forgive the houses of the ruined roofs and basements.
Bless the bright loud screen of the television.
And the actors in reality tv: forgive them.
Bless their discoveries and their indulgences.

Bless the orchard's scent of bruised apples.
Forgive the haze of gnats who love the fragrance.
And the feral cats: forgive their trampling paws
across the parsley of spring and its fretty wants,
aloof as the honeysuckle's casual lust.

Bless the mother her imperfection in dying,
forgive her paleness in the yet attractive world.
Forgive the father of the imperfect intersection
and the car unaware of the missing stop sign.
Forgive the town council who knew it was down,
and who knew of accidents before, and had done nothing:

bless their imperfections and their quiet rooms.
And the blessed imperfection of the berry trees
whose leaves drop in heart shapes to cool the green down.
The berries later who will stain the roads, forgive them:

let the archetype of fruit with an interior seed
keep its temperamental future, always dreaming, dreaming.
Forgive the center of the berry, with its fertile gift,
and its history of pattern, burning off the parent flower.
It is sorry to admit it: let it go, let it go.

And the cats who stare at nothing in the evening: leave them.
Forgive the cats, overlook the fact of squirrels in the attic.
Bless the imperfections of the trailing world.
Bless what's left of it, crestfallen, havoc-filled, pretty,
thirsty at the core and tortured with blooms.

# THE SPACE OF WHETHER GOD EXISTS

I want perfection, but the flesh resists.
The garden tulips wrenched out by mischief
into the space of whether God exists.

Carnelian tulips rise in softened fists,
their petals bruised to brilliance in the leaf.
I'd love perfection, but the flesh resists.

Red mouths undo engagements with a kiss
(mouths apple-red, cliché as Eden-grief)
into the space of whether God exists.

A metaphor, the tulip's short-term bliss?
Exhausted petals: Eve's *undone* motif.
I'd love perfection—but the flesh resists,

and tulips grow to ruin, and life insists.
Bulbs sleeping underground for this burst brief
into the space of whether God exists.

I haven't used the rhyme-word *atheist*.
Lord, I believe; Help me Thou my unbelief.
I'd love perfection but the flesh resists
into the space of whether God exists.

# FACTS

Facts! How beautiful you are! I'd rather not be vulnerable
for anything, for anyone; that's a dream.
Instead of entitlement, America, how about this: love,
desire, for diversity in all things,

for anything, for any anyone; that's a dream
I remember from childhood.
Desire for diversity. In all things
bright and beautiful, from the horse's

—I remember from childhood—
evidence-based galloping, how hard and fast, how
bright and beautiful. *From the horse's
mouth*, we say when we're sure,

evidence-based. Galloping, how hard and fast, how
sure we are with our beliefs. *From your
mouth*, we say when we're sure,
*to God's transgender ear*, then hope.

Sure we are, with our beliefs, from your
anti-science-based magic. Yet a fetus sings purely
to God's transgender ear. Then hope
that won't be lost, won't petrify to fear, can resist

anti-science-based magic. Yet a fetus sings purely
instead of entitlement. America, how about this? Love
that won't be lost, won't petrify to fear, can resist.
Facts! How beautiful you are! I'd rather not be vulnerable.

# SUMMER OF DEAD ANIMALS

Then the cat killed a bird, the wings
a little twisted and shot through
with a gorgeous blue. The raccoon
on one side in the heat, until we rolled
the stiff chenille body
into a small metal trough.
When his claws hit the galvanized metal
they made a whisper of a sound.
If I were a poet who could do Romanticism,
that sound from the claws of the animal—
raccoons with their
famously hypersensitive paws—
I'd take from that sound
something about culpability.
What could a good poet make of this terrible thing?
Also: motionless vole in the clover—
and then two mice, their pink feet
tiny, as tapered and delicate
as pale pink sorrel
in the wet grass—
the fox limping out of the meadow.
The dead squirrel's smoky mouth upturned
and open, a poor thing in unenlightened dirt.
We carried him too, I promise you,
to the woods, and put the soft and rolling stuff
beneath the shade of green things.
I want you to know how little he weighed.
A better writer would not have to write that,
reader, but I've been discouraged
by this failure to connect what is mine
with the words. Oh for the bright before.
I can't do anything to help the unfeathering,
the pressing hungers that leave
each trembling thing abandoned.

When the cat shapes his eyes
to the almond and accusing yellow,
I have even less to say. And each day,
I wake to it, a gift in better hands.

# DEATH VISITS THE GARDEN

There he is among the gradual ferns.
The coneflowers are a purple darkened
in the sky's gray, and him nearby.
He is putting his whole hood
over the hyssop, lowering his bone nose
for the scent. *Can you get the fragrance?*
I ask and he says *Not enough.*

We are familiars; we know each other.
He fits in among the livid daisies,
and nervous birds don't mind that he putters
among the seed under the birdfeeder
fingering the milkweed, touching the basil,
raising that articulate hand bunched with green
to his skull again, inhaling.

*Oh I love this*, he says, *I love this*,
folding basil leaves into his cloak.
*Pick some weeds*, I say. *Make yourself useful.*
Green violet plants stagger the grass.
Bees roll in serial clover.
From high limbs, birds insist on something.
*I am useful*, he argues, and in that wild moment
I see his armies of bone buried in the field.

## AMONG THE GOSPEL TREES THE ONLY MOVING THING

A red bird preserves a note in its beak
on the cusp of now,

picturing the rich gap it will fill
when the beak opens, and the air volunteers,

as if nature will respond to such trying.
This appeals to my twenty-first century loneliness.

That will be the last mention of the eye
of an observer who becomes so unimportant

against these curves and these presumptions,
these roots growing out of an earth

somehow imperative and nonverbal,
somehow inarticulate in typeface, but still pictorial,

this unrelenting yard illustrative of physics
out of the grand books of thought.

Among the evidence of tree, a breeze about to be,
and beneath this: a fleshy kneeling toward belief.

These forms are not tortured in bearing, in burdening,
though rounded under the bird's about-to-be richness,

human thought a rough technology of skin and brain,
atriums beneath the ribbons of good news

the gospel trees suspend, if their wet bursts of fruit
are evidence of love. If anything were here

it would want to turn toward a chamber of belief,
as any infant ear turns toward the new world,

as pure as fish rolling in the afterthought of waves,
lush as a deep eye, like the horse's eye,

which is playful because it looks to know something.
If there are mortals there while the horse looks out,

as the playful eye moistens against the impact of air,
they become pure image on the retina, the horse

lowering its head to focus on what's close.
He lets down the pliant curve of the bowing head.

Among the gospel trees the only moving thing
—beside the fish in the sea, turning in their sleep,

and the horse-rich field, and their focusing eyes,
and their ocular nerves, and their praying manes,

and the horizon against which everything is perceived,
and the shifting field of vision, from left to right,

and you listener, if I risk that chance,
to imagine for a moment your existing there—

were the bird's soft muscles, holding the passage,
about to trust to the open of air

what it would sing, the burst of dependence all *tweet* and *tweet*
as the song moves over its diminishing yield.

Maybe this moved too: the human heart, atrium a-waiting,
all veins strung up with its oohs and aahs,

it intrudes by taking red blood to the chambers,
these provisional zones of pass and pass.

# SEVEN WORDS

Forgive them, for they don't know what they do.
Blood, veins, infinity, the garden, your words
in metaphor: the whole story rises dark blue
in the trees' green burdens, drenched with voice.

Blood, veins, infinity, the garden, your words
all dissolve, like the story itself, to myth
in the trees. Green burdens drenched with voice
blur the stories, insist and transform, bright leaves.

All dissolve, like the story itself, to myth.
A million habits arrange and rearrange
blur. The stories insist and transform bright leaves
beneath which, birds preening: forlorn, lost shapes.

A million habits arrange and rearrange,
provide: to shift, adjust, put right, perfect.
Beneath which birds, preening forlorn lost shapes,
is the first tree, the dark encroachment and the rest?

Provide: to shift, adjust, put right, perfect.
In metaphor the whole story rises dark blue.
Is the first tree the dark encroachment? And the rest?
Forgive them, for they don't know what they do.

# WHEN THE DOVE FLEW OVERHEAD,

                                         it marked
the edge of a circle, split into the raked sky a seam
I thought I saw, and given the right atmosphere,
would travel through. Do I believe?

The sky was widened slightly, as it widens
at the tip of threatened churches,
and the spire rises higher
so the deity is nearer, so can be a better listener,

there where language speaks in ... forgetfulness?
Forgiveness? A language of insistence, of distance,
to match the kind of language the dove cooed as it flew
its zoology of feathers,

and the pressure, like foreboding,
of its quills against a sky. My eye's insistence on it.
When the dove flew the arc overhead,
it marked the edge of something,

and internally I noted its incessance on my eye.
It whistled something sparse and bright,
an increment of grieving, of the bird's fear,
a cataract in miniature of leavings.

Because he was alone.
A flock of geese will migrate
to their applause of wings, aerodynamic union
who fly toward some hot love or to some climate,

all together. The howl bark of flight into a migratory *V*,
a pattern they agree upon because they know their world.
They turn away from air,
betray the air

in pleasure of their pattern,
wherein they feel the buoyancy of worth.
Unlike the single dove,
off-balance into thin air between pinfeather and earth.

The hot arc of goodbye through which it flew
its thread into a sky so unprepared,
it didn't look to care,
it couldn't have cared less if bird remained.

But I was watching then, to see if bird,
untumbled from the air,
might be received in tree, by tree, or limb,
welcomed by something loving there,

maybe that maple by the border there,
where any day mosquitoes will be cruel, and prick for glee
to bleed us in a metaphor for leaving the first world,
for all this silent treatment, this itch of uselessness.

At the first twitch of his flight, I caught his gray ingenious,
and in my stopping to admire,
I tried to read the richness,
to hesitate amid the language he might scratch in adoration,

to see what charm his runes would tell the sky,
or otherwise,
to see if clouded sky would love him as he rose,
so loves us, too. So that as the bird flew

his tender body toward an incoherent blue,
I wished an answer there against the dizziness of air,
against the imperceptible, I made myself aware.
And something like a gray bird did appear, then disappear.

# AN INCOMPLETE ENCYCLOPEDIA
# OF HAPPINESS AND UNHAPPINESS

An incomplete encyclopedia of happiness
would have an entry on you
and a map of the walk you took when you were ten,
jingling your allowance and imagining a kingdom.
It would have a list of places to go for ice cream
and a compendium of the naturally sweet fruits,
their hues of flesh arranged on a color chart,
and types of candies in alphabetical order.

It would have an illustration of the angle of an infant
held in the cradle of arm, and an explanation
of the relationship of the word *Elysium*
to the broad arc the robin flies
beneath the seemingly perfect
—almost emerald—
leaves of the summer, when the heart beats from joy,
when it's almost too much, really.

The companion volume on unhappiness
starts earlier than it should, and contains
statistics on loss in blurry, mite-sized type.
There's an article on that time the popular girl
squirted ketchup on your new shirt, the one
your mother worked six extra days to pay for,
near the entry on Children in War Zones,
just to emphasize the shame of selfishness.

There's a fold-out map of innocence lost,
and a hierarchy of illness
that runs off the top of the page.
Under a bibliography of missed opportunities,
a relief map using contour lines and shading
registers the exact moments
you said the wrong thing,
the utterly wrong thing.

You'll find the Venn diagram of *war* and *wisdom*
under *Inexplicable Human Acts, W.*
There's a series of color plates:
one of Adam and Eve in a paradise,
one of McDonald's,
and one of Adam and Eve entering McDonald's.
And the appendix on political correctness
explains why none of that is funny.

The editor is up nights, compiling and revising
everything ever done or made
or imagined or hoped for,
everything bright and glazed
or dulled by use, or rubbed away
or fought for, or thrown or thrown at
or razed or constructed
or conceived of, or created, or traveled

or found, or glued together with sticks
or woven on a loom
or ripening, or run from, or planted
or trampled or rotted or lived with
or ruined, or feared, or endured,
everything believed and debunked, or believed and lost,
everything learned and everything forgotten,
including the incomplete encyclopedia,

including the editor's research, his days compiling,
his nightmares about the stalled elevator,
a chart of his wife's depression,
a graph of expenses for his kids' birthday parties,
his fantasy about laying out Tim Hunter,
his love of cards, his fear of swans,
his father's regret and his mother's voice, singing,
all this unhappiness, all this happiness.

## MAKING SMALL TALK, THE CASHIER AT THE GROCERY INADVERTENTLY CREATES A RELIGION

Passing the pears over the scanner, she says
*These are beautiful. Look at the markings!*
And: *I don't know the story of where they're from.*
*But I believe they are just right.*
And passing the figs:
*So complex, what's on the inside.*
*Everything worthwhile has a kind of mystery.*
*I don't bother with it more than that.*
The chévre in its paper, rolled
and taped, she handles with care.
*I'll put that on top. With delicate things*
*its best to be careful. What is it?*
she asks. When I tell her goat cheese,
she smiles. *Everything,* she says,
*that partakes of the grasses*
*will taste of the grasses. Everything*
*that partakes of the earth...*
*and in all this rain we've been having...*
passing the berries across,
waving the delicate wafers by the scanning eye.
*I just let the day unfold,* she says
waving the bottle of wine across,
*and try to dress accordingly.*

# THE GREAT DISAPPOINTMENT

*At Ascension Rock in Whitehall, New York, on the night of October 22, 1844,*
*ten thousand Millerites (named for their leader William Miller) gathered to wait*
*for Christ's return—a night known thereafter as the Great Disappointment.*

To wait for Christ, we stood scoured clean
in cotton robes, all cotton-wrapped, sure,
upturned. We'd scrubbed this temporary earth
for evidence, and Miller rendered Daniel perfect
fact: the beasts, the numbers read as promise,
the angels' tiny trumpet blasting *you're forgiven.*

Lord, for all mistakes I ask we be forgiven.
Our dreaming of the world wrenched clean,
dissolved for us, was vanity. I promise
to accept flawed rests as rapt, sure
notes, a theme with many rests, a perfect
grace on perfect air—imperfect, brittle earth,

this counterfeit reversal. False sky above fake earth,
its tender scenery that we were given for
the first true world when wonder made imperfect
all perfection. The stupid girl and Adam, unclean
bodies restless, hair, arms, legs, wrapped, sure.
Scared. Out of luck for breaking the first promise.

Gates shut then. Grief, this compromise:
a muddled, deep-befuddled people trudging earth,
shaping flawed lines in braided form toward rapture.
(In this poem, six: a perfect number, so, forgiven?)
Then at Ascension we spoke into clean
pure air, *Knock Knock! Perfection! Now!* And *Perfect!—*

but we remained. Bad planning? An imperfect
understanding of the prophet Daniel's promise?
Miller saw Rome as a vain lion; I watched a mother clean
her child and fold him in her cloak, saying *On earth,*

*the holy land's a door, a gift; we're not forgiven.*
The door stayed locked. In imperfection trapped. Shore

vanishes, old enchantments fade. The withdrawn rapture
deflates the God balloon. I wanted to be perfect,
to rise in yeasty faith through air, forgiven,
the ghost myth making good on every promise
offered: each prophecy and wish, and earth
scrubbed of us, scoured of stain, so clean

it burns. No dice. What now? Hope again for rapture
on this earth with hungry kids, with nothing but this perfect
sense of loss? God, come clean with some proof, and be forgiven.

# SLEEP

As morning yawns polite goodbyes to last night's imperfection,
My sleepless body curtsies to the princess, imperfection.

Each day I try to build a house that, nightly, fails to stand.
There is no jeweled castle worth this sweat, this imperfection.

My sleep's church flush with true-believers, tousled weary sheep
observing nightly worship with me, Abbess Imperfection.

Where is the lightened spring that, rinsing, hastens all the bloom?
This season's rains beget the drench of crisis: imperfection.

Within these English couplets I'll essay an Urdu line.
My pencil too American to dismiss imperfection.

At 6 a.m. a blue jay's cranky beauty, full of noise.
His tail alone was fashioned from his lies, his imperfection.

I try to keep the garden from entering the poem,
But bursting vines will intertwine in bliss/imperfection.

The stray black cat is focused on his torture of a thrush
Until I fight to save it. The score: one less imperfection?

Rude, reckless cats will torture birds, and reckless dogs will cats;
Their guiltless afternoons of naps reminisce imperfection.

Wakes poorly, one drinks poorly, sleeps poorly; doesn't dream.
I wouldn't be surprised to learn we piss imperfection.

I'd love a rest in quiet air, to dream a given name.
Not each night's blatant baptismal abyss, imperfection.

Unbaptized by sleep's blessings, I'll aim to remain unnamed,
a shadowy cartographer. My atlas: Imperfection.

# THE FOX

The fox didn't know it was tame.
I fed the fox; I provided the environment.
*Just don't hurt the cats*, I warned.

The fox was unaware it was tame.
It sat on the deck when it snacked on what I gave him.
Beneath the deck small birds pecked at the grasses.

The fox has pretty black legs and a red, curt body.
Sweet ambivalence! And with such sharp teeth!
The fox behaved like a fox, ignored

my one request, so I don't feed him anymore.
What are the signs of the world falling?
1) I don't open the door. 2) A dry mouth,

a parched tongue. 3) The hunger.
4) I disappear. It is colder as the season changes.
Whatever provided the daily bread no longer provides;

the hungry birds are bound for a thinning. Fear flutters
the scattered moles. Even my beautiful fox has bones,
severe and sour in the lamentable, angry,

exacting eye of autumn. At the root of the tale,
regret shifts her legs in bitter steps; she pretends not to notice
the languishing everywhere. Take care. Be well!

Bon voyage! Something or someone has turned the head
on the neck of giving. The fox had no idea
what it was to be wild, to be abandoned to wilderness.

## THE PERENNIALS

Underneath is planetary dark,
a stupor of languid tubers, heedless,
lax, careless, irreligious—interrupted again

by light, followed by a series of disappointments.
Oh give up with your amnesia of springtime.
Winter's eyes ice life transfigured,

happy to be dead again, in the fine, dry
hard, bitter, honest, authentic dirt. Who cares?
Whatever you like, whatever.

Having survived the tender perjury in staggered petals,
the fuss and haste of beauty, the distraction
of the sky's adoring, inconsistent face.

Oh God. Oh God.
The whole screaming mastery of resuscitation, the bloom
thrashing the wind with delicate angers, lying through her teeth.

The blossom is an object about to be drained of faith.
The upper world demands and exhausts for *pretty*.
Spring is galling: its parasol of brevity, its lacquer of belief.

## THE CAT

The old cat turns by curving
what's left of his body
beyond the careless trees. Does it ache,

each twinge and cramp, to wander in hunger,
ever fruitless at eye-level?
Across the lawn the sunlight, having come all that way

is giving up.
Now the deadpan fox has changed his course.
The twitch and bristle of instinct,

tender as murder, my god, and next,
under the mangy strands of wind, under the chill,
animals are sources, little meats!

Let the loving deaths begin,
let out the ashes, the brocade of bone,
layer atop layer of material released,

the veins colder, the whole skinflint world.
Aren't you tired of it all, aren't you weary,
cat, having to place one foot after the other

towards evening's stingy gristle? No comment.
Neither the cat nor the grass he bothers
can recognize any largeness of his life,

the creature's stubborn desire
to find its commonplace, its eternal,
as if anything ever adds up to poetry.

The sun's gone now. Bleak forfeit.
Old habits pacing, the wind rearranging its *yes*,
the X-ray moon revising the evening's bones.

# JAPONICA RATIONALIZES THE POSSIBILITY OF A HEAVEN

If heaven is white and not madness then the sky would refract such clarity blue.

If it is right and not wild or unrelenting then I can wait in depleting peace.

If it is possible to enter the kingdom of such unmadness then why not?

By which I mean heaven if it is truly hovering and not dishonest.

White for purity like the kind meek offerings of the sun.

So therefore blue to my sight because of distance and refraction.

Blue known again from a humming novelty, from freshness.

All right so there.

So therefore my patience and tenacity can seem invasive.

The archetypal sea green japonica weary and insistent for something's sake.

As it chokes the ground because if so why not try to cover every square foot.

Requesting through transpiration the love note back.

Revealing through blossom the formula of yes.

Bestowing the hope of yes indeed to the dumb sucking root.

Why not body forth out of the desire to be blessed?

The origin of ache in a whorl of petal and reddish fruit.

Glossy, growing easily on graves because why not?

In spring a burst of absolute certainty suspended, followed by misgivings.

# RABBIT AND HAWK

In the interval, an element and its hostile equivalent.
The hawk flies up with a difficult freight,
then rabbit substance drops in soft failure. I see

a puny spectacular, the ooze and filtrate,
red gush mechanics of vanishing.
Dead rabbit eyes emptying out, released into the wild,

and it felt like a kiss, unloved. *So this is all*, I thought.
The god apparatus distracted in reverie,
The god project agitated elsewhere, a spark:

thinking of a god, I make a god,
a larva god shivering in fuels,
waxing in a god lathe, turning in truant resins.

Does he resent my missing his presence?
The window frame hive body, the mind's sharpened tools.
I had catalogued your restless flowers,

spun your birds into dimension, navigated
each tooth and feather, each difficult beadwork eye
above your half-tone death yard, your acute, excitable

accelerant dusk. It took layers of need to sew you up, god thimble,
sullen, intractable threads, brood materials, your death love!
The unwieldy scours my blood, your incognito split open

as the hawk pivots its fibrous wits at the pencil's edge
above the limited world's meats and pelts,
all perceiving motor, optic nerve, dead hunger.

# YOU SHOULD PUT A DONKEY IN YOUR POEM

You should put a donkey in your poem
and it will get probably the job done.
It will carry the stones that were in the way
up the hill, and it might stop now and then,
but the stones—which are now at the bottom of the hill
will be carried and will arrive.

I mean a donkey like the donkey of Auden's Ischia,
the donkey who will lean against a wall
striped with sun. Now I see the donkey has eyelashes.
It will accept its fate and clop mildly.
It will lean and rest, but when it has rested, it will continue.
It doesn't distract with ornament. On it goes.

And I can imagine it would be devout. Such a donkey,
a donkey like Auden's, is not beautiful but it is efficient.
It has purpose: by being in the narrative, I begin to observe
the charming streets of Ischia, the sun, a place
where a useful, solid animal, with satisfying eyes,

can labor and still be charming. I see donkey-brown eyes,
and a stout body leaning, with an imaginary woven basket
filled with stones. I was not heading this way,
but now I think this is beautiful, the donkey and Ischia.
I get sentimental. This is one of the biggest problems with poetry.

# WE COULD HAVE FUCKED, BUT TWITTER

I'm not trying to be unkind, I promise. You
stare at your laptop like the moon.
Twitter doesn't help us fix the world. We know it's true.

You wanted me to take off this dress, and I withdrew,
naked and longing in the dark bedroom.
I'm not trying to be unkind, I promise you.

Outside: the meadow flowers, the scented yew.
Inside: the doom scroll's ache, the web's perfume.
Twitter doesn't help us fix the world. We know it. True,

we tweet to help…. we tweet for… tweet to—
I don't even know. To pass the afternoon?
I'm not trying to be unkind, I promise you.

Offline I'd have licked every bit of you,
pulled up my skirt in the men's bathroom.
Twitter doesn't help us fix the world we know. It's true:

this villanelle won't either. Poem here, meme there, review
your tweets, and check who @ed you. Resume.
I'm not trying to be unkind; I promise you

a kiss, if you … glance up? The art of losing you
is a cinch to master. Boom.
I'm not trying to be unkind, I promise you.
Twitter doesn't help us fix the world. We know it's true.

## WHILE TRANSLATING A BIOGRAPHY,
## I FALL IN LOVE WITH YOU AGAIN

How the young girl in this biography
would write exaggerated letters to her grandmother,
thrilled by the professor's dark looks, his Italian
brooding, his meager body running on lost energies
like a worn cat. His pockets torn, she wrote,
because he was so devoted to poverty and to ideas,
on which he survived, as if breathing through his mind.
The young dream their ideals into being,
and court them, as you walked behind me
those years before we graduated college,
on the otherwise empty street,
when I dropped what I thought was a 20 dollar bill
and skipped around to chase it,
and there you were.
I needed that 20. I was trying to get to the bus,
to get out of town because your dark looks were on my mind
too much,
your poverty, your starved, insistent sex,
the narrow silence in which we'd drift,
a soft nightfall inside the body.
I turned to chase the bill and ran into you,
and you said something. I don't remember.
The bus arrived.

Even as I lowered myself to the coach seat
and looked out the window on the highway to Columbus
where I hoped a mall there would cleanse my desire,
I felt the last glint of my willpower leave me
like late sun along a damaged bee's wing.
Love is amnesia, you forget
that you were ever unbeautiful,
that you were ever unkind, that life
didn't surround you like the curved and carelessly lovely
petals of a flower.
What's the point of petals, anyway?
A soft compulsion stretching out toward an invisible,

a foolish idea touching its cage.
To translate, you study context: her father did not approve.
He was forbidden, then.
He was like a breathing god, courting her.
He showed her the museums of Naples and Rome.
Once he touched her shoulder and her heart moved faster.
The space behind her ears got warm,
and the pupils of her eyes widened. More light
entered the retina. She couldn't forget him,
even when her father demanded.
*It will not diminish*, she wrote her grandmother:
*non si affievolirà*. Or *not weaken*, maybe she means. Or *not let go*.
Maybe in the context of the letter, it's more like:
*it will not let me go*.
Translating means betraying for love of ideas,
or finding perfect fidelity,
or working to practically efface yourself,
or all three at once.
The bus took me back home that evening
and how pretty was each small turn in the road.
My body was a softness over bones, like now
under the small, stiff windows.
*I love you*, something said inside me, in whatever language,
and I went home to all my books.

# THE LETTING GO

Somehow I managed to let go of you.
You said you loved me deeply, but it was
not true, not true, not true, not true, not true.

The bees enjoy the pollens they accrue,
but I'm forgetting you with each day's buzz,
somehow. I managed to let go of you.

Regret's a dark, sweet nectar I fly through.
I'll make of it a honey labeled *Was
Not True, Not True, Not True, Not True, Not True.*

Let's inscribe those two words as a tattoo:
blurred inks, indelible as my heart thaws.
Somehow I managed. To let go of you,

I'm pouring water on this crazy glue,
this airtight seal, whose lifetime guarantee's
not true. *Not true! Not true! Not true! Not true!*

my heartbeat says. Oh fuck its point of view,
insistent muscle, pumping out red laws.
Somehow I managed to let go of you.
(Not true, not true, not true, not true, not true.)

# The Sin Sonnets

_____

# ICARUS

The great mistake was that, in fashioning
the winged parts he fit to my backbone,
my father shaped his love (but that alone)
to wax unstrengthened by a thickening.
Thus lighter, they would mold to feathered shape
quick. Overnight. By light, our instruments
would hinge two human birds from their laments
of labyrinth to open sky's escape.

Or maybe the sun knew I wished to clutch
her private skirt of warmth, and hotly grieves
to find that human want and human touch
might fly so close. If everyone could see
what I perceived when I approached that much
of God, the sky would fill with human leaves.

# PRIDE

A poem to hold bold ideas of free will
should use a form once supple and elastic;
perhaps the rules of sonnet are so drastic
fulfilling them might render free will still.
Yet, if in forming mortals, one consents
to cage the sin of Pride within constraints,
one could avoid Icarus's complaints.
His father's crafting he misrepresents:

it was divinity of wax and feather,
to liberate them from the Minotaur,
from maze's curbing form. His thoughtful words,
"Avoid the sun," might have kept them together.
But pride provided pride, for son to soar
too briefly in the infinite of birds.

## KING AHAB

The ruling limits of a form may kill
a bad desire, curb imperfect thought,
so that someone behaves as someone ought,
though human cadences beat with free will.
I cannot say this worked for me re: greed.
I coveted the neighbor's land of vines.
My conscience might have stayed between the lines,
but Jezebel, my wife, fulfilled my need.
My need? Well, need, or want...I didn't covet
my neighbor's wife, I wanted just his land
which annexed my land. Jezebel would love it
if matters could have gone the way we planned.

But neighbor's land and neighbor's wife the same,
though I pretended to misunderstand this.
I'm good at that; I'm adept at pretending
misunderstanding, that's how rules get tame—
You might note how this sonnet's form expands with
my insatiable needs, the lines not ending,
for, as I wanted land, I want more spaces
than sonnet form permits me here to use.
The rhymes that force me into little twos
coerce bright ideas into brief places.

It's fitting, really, this free will debate
applies so clearly to all I've acquired—
I know it's wrong to plunder real estate.
Jezebel and I might have been inspired
to remain in the first home we desired
if we knew where we'd be when we retired.

# GREED

Desire won't submit to rationing.
Or is it: rationing won't quit desire?
The problem's whether form controls the fire
or whether wanting ruins everything.
The heavens simulate an ordered plan
where planets, luminous, seem to trace paths,
to flash their dreamy greens and blues in maths,
but how they rotate in attention, span
a wandering of wants, of deprivations.

The word *planet* comes from the Greek: *to wander.*
Under these spheres, we reproduce their lacks,
and hover in erratic constellations.
Thus swerving, planet drifts form night's bright blurs, or
when they stray too far, the sky's deep blacks.

# (LUST)

A sinning voice may spread the blame, and whine
that if God made each pattern that exists,
that humans are allowed each happiness
(but lust is not a passion of design).

So Pasiphae to David (see below)
might blame her lust on the Greek god Poseidon
(or Daedalus, who made her shape to hide in).
Such passion was not passion apropos,

though her lust was incredible, and how!
It flavored her as wormwood flavors absinthe.
(You may submit a different exegesis.)
She had the craftsman craft a wood she-cow
(it was a better project than his labyrinth)
lust's text enclosed in she-cow parenthesis.

# PASIPHAE AND DAVID

"You lusted for a bull." David accuses,
"as animals will want to screw their own,
plus you deceived King Minos, whose rough throne
your bull-beridden behind still misuses.
"That's so," the other thoughtfully replies,
"I did not force Uriah's wife toward blame,
order her husband destroyed in my name.
I only loved a bull in my disguise—

—But how I craved that beast of gust and thrust."
"Yes, Bathsheba's breasts glistened, like a sea,
so that I had to swim her, just because."
Lust's thespians perform a play of trust;
by drama's end they'll bow to destiny,
though neither one will merit much applause.

# FORM

Imperfect world, its history of excuses—
Perfection was pre-bible and pre-myth.
There'd be no Cain or Pasiphae herewith,
or Icarus, with whom we compare bruises
of falling, of temptation, of sin city.
Their stories are our stories, like Snow White
who, of the proffered apple took a bite
(she too found bright fruit poisonously pretty.)

Sin's bliss exists alike in myth and tale,
and though these sonnets act as an embrace,
they cannot fix what isn't fixable;
Outside strict lines sin wanders, out of scale.
Though free will may choose balance, might find grace,
sin makes imbalance irresistible.

# CORDELIA

A father's hope, like sonnets, will confine
the family's love. Within this guided fence,
he measured words to figure innocence,
though my sisters fit lies to his design.
But I made all my truths as one makes wine,
to clarify his palate, or incense,
which permeates the air as a fragrance
and softens with its sweetness truth unkind.

If I knew then that as the play's sequence
continued, like a formal poem's guidelines,
our fate would breed a motif of disaster,
I would have, to his pattern, truth condensed.
To undo design might have been divine.
But I am not. His rage caused Rage to fester,

to sprout a tail, caudate
that circled him as would the Saturn's ring
or serpent's twining diamonds, patterning

his madness firm as fate
to suffocate my Lear, tighten him blind.
Pure rages we are helpless to unwind.

# SIN

Still overrule is thwarted by invention.
Though not so in the sad case of Lear's daughter:
her truth in love did not save her from slaughter.
Though cruelty was not King Lear's intention,
the seven sins account for much that's cruel:
*pride, anger, envy, greed, lust, sloth, excess*
(well, *gluttony*. But that won't fit unless
I mold the word to fit within the rule.)
Control works gracefully in sonnet's mold.
If ethics might control the seven sins,

then free will wouldn't blossom for the worse.
Iambics won't let disorder unfold.
But poem is heartbeat and strange blood within;
is wildness better suited to free verse?

# CAIN

I didn't bring the best fruit—that was clear,
dragging my basket wildly on the dirt.
My brother's eyes pure, empty of the hurt
of envy's prick I'd feel again. In fear,
my arms outstretched to Him, for want of love
I'd ask, human-thin voice above the bleats
of animals half-snorting in the heat.
He knew my bleak insides that wished to shove
Abel away.

                He would know everything.
So why should he not eat my lemons bruised?
So why should he berate my bitter hate?
My heart is traced to the abandoning
of Eden for this place He's made, confused
as fathers are, and I recriminate.

# ENVY

Sin makes this second world imperfect stuff,
so filled with countless human misdirection,
but that's our circumstance, our imperfection,
and we may have to leave it soon enough—

Yet like the envy Cain felt for his brother,
I feel a covetousness for the garden,
if such a thing existed. You must pardon
my momentary lusting for the other:

that's part of our exile, such imperfection.
Please pardon me that doubt, that's also part
of our imperfect status, and this poem,
which tries to write about it with affection.
And then forgive this envious, lost heart
whose words seek quite imperfectly for home.

## SLOTH

Though loving liberation within tension,
Cain overdoes his freedom with his sins,
and breaks the margin of love's disciplines,
to float, a boat unmoored, on sin's suspension
bridge, over *Lake Sloth: Lagoon Affliction*.
Sloth's a horse latitude of two strong features,
*acedia* : uncaring to God's creatures,
*tristitia*: with nothing of conviction,
a sorrow becomes sorrow of despair.
There's Judas, too, who saw no use repenting,
together in the boat they both are helming.
They look out on blank space, and heat, and air,
and steer toward nothing. It's so unrelenting.
The dormancy of sloth is overwhelming.

# WILDS

In sonnets, wilderness might disappear,
grown weary with the too-strict iamb,
make form the Thailand to its once-Siam,
deputize silhouette to reign severe,
to outline regions wilderness deserts.
There'd be heartbeat beyond our unwild dreams
but nothing beating there.
                                    Between extremes
of order firm, where strange disorder flirts,
and shows her skirts, we find our wilderness,
our paradise: severe, austere, chaotic.
A human overflows with contradiction,
an imperfection poetry should address,
synchronously pacific and neurotic.
It's similarly hopeless in nonfiction.

# ADAM

Was Paradise, our wilderness, enough?
(Khayyam would put it differently in song.)
Tempted, my Eve transgressed and called the bluff
and from her gluttony we both went wrong.

It's possible to say, in her defense,
*the apple shimmered like a promise kept—*
that *wanting was not disobedience—*
But God did not agree. We slept; He wept.

When I look back I wish expedience
had been our stronger suit, and not temptation.
I wish we had used doubt, some common sense
to warn us that snakes alter destination.
Such doubt did not exist in Paradise.
Though it defines us in this compromise.

## ECHO

The great mistake was that, in fashioning
a poem form to hold ideas of free will,
the rules and limits of the form may kill.
Desire won't submit to rationing.
A sinning voice may spread the blame and whine:
"She lusted for a bull." David accuses.
Freedom in form means one makes no excuses.
A Father's hope, like sonnets, will confine—
still, overrule is thwarted by invention—
(Cain didn't bring the best fruit—that was clear.)
Sin makes this second world imperfect stuff.
Though loving liberation within tension,
in sonnets, wilderness might disappear.
Was Paradise, our wilderness, enough?

# The Space of Whether God Exists

_____

*Where does the edge of the canvas end
and the edge of the world begin?*

—DOUGLAS FOGLE

# WAKING IN THE SPACE OF WHETHER GOD EXISTS

Mornings. Sometimes the green of fish belly,
or the pale gray of envelope, opening,
the air within a surprise. I wake up
into the space of whether God exists.

Mornings arrive in the world alone,
in the travel between the first
near-bright horizontal
and the full-on movement. The day nods,
reckoning, realigning.

One can love this. Or
anyway, look with wonder
at the patterns in the living world,
our human walking the awkwardness out
against a landscape, waking, looking

arms waving at air,
arms on hips, hip thrust out,
neck bent, the human form. It's me in this case,

thinking about writing.
See me in there? I'm wondering,
with scratch paper,
into the space of whether God exists.

## HOW FAR IN THE SPACE OF
## WHETHER GOD EXISTS

As far as possible you can walk in the fields
without finding a dotted line, or
the tear in the canvas, turned and stapled
around a wooden frame—see for yourself—
the world goes on and on.

At home in these apprehensions, in this distance,
there aren't breaks in living, noticing,
the real of it—how it continues.
I'm waking now to the real of the world,

how immense and out of my hands.
If I describe it:

>    [And here would be description, declaration;
>    what separates the *it*
>    from the paint or language in which I describe *it*.
>    The *this* in italics says how different.

As in:

over here, the *this*.
Above us, *this, blue* and
*all-knowing* or
*blue, indifferent*.] There goes the human,

walking out to the room of the world,
gazing the limits.
Where the photograph looks, where the painting
looks, the poem looks. It's very close.

## ATTEMPTING VERISIMILITUDE IN THE
## SPACE OF WHETHER GOD EXISTS

The axis shifts when I try to lay my brush on it,

the axis flips the field like a crossed eye.
In the story I am telling, in the story I am trying to tell,

there's a bird suddenly aware
of the human being, and then the human being

suddenly aware of the bird. Swift.
My eye to the edge of this circle sharpens,

marks another of the many, light eases to dark
in another kind of meaning-making.

And the bird's trill is an act of saying
something of the landscape of being a bird,

and a human ear absorbs the song as declaration
or experience, and marks the distance between the two as fluid,

shifting, impossible to re-make, and tiring as a bed of moss.
On a dare I would lie down there, in that moss I just imagined,

on what separates us, the axis between *this* and *that*—
the space between knowing and wondering, seeing and believing,

or writing the real: to hold in ink actual doubt—
and imagine the days understandable, literal,

apprehensible in words. The bird has stopped; it hears my approach.

## DRINKING COFFEE IN THE SPACE
## OF WHETHER GOD EXISTS

The fear of drafting is:
        [written in words, noise
        scratched on the semi-white
        of paper]
that one is responsible for
all that is the space of whether God exists. It's me in this case
[see me in here?] This means
        [for a start]
I'm wondering about what comes first,
and how to write this
across what's noticed after,

apprehending as my camera eye weakens
so the sunlight
        [first]
like a pencil, strokes halfway across the gravel
        [second]
posed like
        [something I'll get to later].
And looking up then, I have to write
into the space of whether God exists.

[Something I'll get to later.]

Oh, the whole outside and its mad betrayal into the eye.
        —the water for the coffee starting to boil now—
        —the good outside world making a short promise—
        giving something—I might return such love—such sentiment—
This works if it would hold still. Everything I see:

        the tree, half-still and leaning out, the absent sky
with its erasures and repetitions, or below me the leaves,
and a caterpillar too small
for my first or second notice—

the day now sentences and syntaxes,
and writhes in brevities of green, and I fail again.

The day resists my punctuation
in tiny alterations, its hem sewing up
and then unsewn, the fairy tale of telling and retold,
and won't return my gaze, although the caterpillar
       [now that I notice]


has paradigms, has models,
has intricate design.

It's fitting we should have a thirst for deepening dimension.
I look into a space for what it yields.
And now I see the caterpillar's pattern echoes peacock:
a swarm of eyes in feathered browns and whites,
repeated visions on his segments, soft as dust.

## A STORM MOVES INTO THE
## SPACE OF WHETHER GOD EXISTS

The storm begins somewhat left of frame—
I felt it there, attending, the short, fast entrance,
tiny gray suspicion, here where we gatherers
investigate our bodies into the daily wait-for-it,

the day, while clouds declare a vantage point, and hold
an ark of water. Where clouds which decorate
another space of whether God exists become
a place where I begin. Or a vanishing point.

It is *something* [emphasis mine] to be human in such rain,
left to the natural in the form of merciful water,
not a cleansing exactly, but it's freshening, changing,
not so much rearranging me as a sloughing something off,

I'm looking up, I'm answering with my senses,
my pitch-dark negatives, bright affirmatives,
my waiting for the finish to it,
my oh-what's-left-of-it, to be in hiding again.

## TRYING IN THE SPACE OF
## WHETHER GOD EXISTS

First the eye, then the increase of senses: the feel of air
on skin, say, giving way to complications:
interior, comprised of body, wishing, in place,
or body, radiant, in motion, sensing.
Or body, troubled, in place,
or body, troubled, in motion, sensing.

The body in a romance in the world,
and the world never commits entirely,
to fluster me with love.
The body hems and haws, hands on hips,
in a field of poppies. [That's me.]
So that a red bloom among red blooms

becomes beauty moving into my eye, and flutters,
fluttering, can't be held. I'm looking at that flower
blooming into a space of whether God exists,
and all these words just irritate the bloom.
The image before the eye dilutes, *oh that*,
I think, but it's too late, having tried to,

trying still, as troubled as a little god, but so much weaker.

## THE HEART TICKS MADLY INTO THE
## SPACE OF WHETHER GOD EXISTS

As when the scenery gets the best of me.
The woods, the houses, set into squares of land,
and inside it, people full of dimension.
Might the human, arm lifted up in all this cartography
—arm scratching at head—hips thrust out—
make a record that is real?

Pencils, protractors ready. Jet knife out. Scissors gape
and think a cut into the image, a shape:
wheat fields *whisper* or *wave in breezes*, depending
on your syntax. Cars *smug in parking spaces*.
Or: *parked* only. *Sweet veins of waters, lament of cloud,*
*blue and arrogant absences*. Getting the idea? Zooming in:
human body in house, head turned to wall
where colors interact on a visual field.

To continue the action: how far inside the human body
—arms scratching, hips thrust—
need I account for, to be true?
How deep within can we operate our figures,
our spirographs and slide rules,
our surly tetrameters?
The heart ticks madly.

# THE PROBLEM OF MUSIC IN THE
# SPACE OF WHETHER GOD EXISTS

Music carves a space in the air
or a series of restless spaces
calling out to be sounded, and then,

how suddenly high is the ceiling
against the persecuted cello, its sweet response
vibrating, pulled to the bow as a wound is pulled, tender,

and the corresponding afternoon now immense,
since where the sound changes in air, the human
may be chastened by dimension.

How suddenly high arcs the ceiling, white around me,
high enough for the lower angels to gather and moan
if they would. Over which the sky tunes up,

bends its pitch to the entire of it, towards little earth,
with its difficult roses, towards the human body,
suspended in air and constantly falling,

who might deny the rush: *I see and hold it*
with declaration: *I declare the world is knowable*
in tercets and quatrains. Oh the human, encircled by things,

always knowing things, and always so wrong,
ever vibrating in the ever vibrating air.

## THE TROUBLE WITH THE
## SPACE OF WHETHER GOD EXISTS

The human moves like a thought,
looking for a place to find a home,
because that's all it can discern of form
among all the other forms, reckless and
inaudible as roses, *which are neither reckless*

*nor inaudible*
       —here the water for the coffee comes to a boil
so there's a little steam, a change in air.
Human, confused—arms scratching head, hip thrust out—
human overdoes its looking, listening, inventing.
That's me. Do you see me here?
Am I in the world when I am writing of it?

The human has painted himself into wondering,
imagined himself part of landscape, at home in a world,
kneeling down now, looking for the sense of it:
looking at the hard, verifiable earth,
peering for the dotted lines the curve where the canvas curls
and is stapled.

This world. Stretched on stretcher bars, gessoed
or luminous: primed with rabbit skin glue
and then a layer of whiting. The world is dimensional.
Impossible. Intoxicate, present, but unverifiable:
awash with flutterings, energetic, but not yet,
as real as the deep wound of the gorgeous that hangs in the eye.

## DRAFTING INTO THE SPACE
## OF WHETHER GOD EXISTS

Now there's a picture to be made—
with words, with paint, with lead, with sketchbook

—that human body in the space of whether God exists.
For that is the thick of it.

All that nonsense that makes us reckless: first bold strokes
toward all that is considered there. What's included.

Vast space green with its starting; unheard-of-flowers
pendant in their present tensing, a virtual yearning

in petal; various animal life; distant, burning field.
          —The water for the coffee starts to boil.—

Into which we place—arms scratching at head, etc—
the human, trying. Protractors ready. Jet knife ready.

Stains, tints and dyes, rabbit skin glue, stretcher bars,
dictionaries, notes, scratches on paper, ready.

Yet unseen: animal asleep and dreaming within the dream, a fire.
Matter falling from a tree limb. Matter remains on the limb.

Something working its way through the bark, too.
The imperfection of such attempts,

so much else I haven't seen yet. Paint, words: everything too still,
everything holds. All should be motion and depth.

What about that sad story over that landline, that line
like an awning in the left corner, near where the frame would go,

dotted, as if to tear, under ornate bare wood with gold streaks.
More scratches on paper. Shifting of protractors. Compasses.

# PHYSICS IN THE SPACE OF
# WHETHER GOD EXISTS

When the poet read and the world
did not appear in the words, but sat back,

green through the window, when the poet read and the world
did not look up or pay attention—out of the corner of its green,

green, the poet read something the world could resist.

It's a question of physics: a world, uninterested,
watches not, and we, interested, watch the world, and a train

will travel purposely, making the passersby
expand in time, in theory as in train $A$

crosses station with passersby $B$, who listen to
poet $C$ read something we can only describe as *knowing*

in the sense of *he seems to know this world, its shape,*
though the emphasis is on he and not the world, and

though the world, as I noted, didn't seem to agree:
it greened up outside the arc of glass, and it statued, yes,

it tossed full leaf and carried sex in seed and distance,
it grew by thin intervals more remote, and scattered and fluttered,

deepened as the absorbing sea, as stiff answers in an early dark,
and the dark itself becoming deeper, knowing its own image

studying, absorbing. The world waved in the night of rain,
a night of punishing rain. Under which, sated, poet $C$

missed the train crossing right in front of the house,
speeding to an infinite calm, arranging, mastering,

making even the poet, who didn't know,
dilate in that moment as example in physics of existence.

Was it imperfect, this voice and the green? Should I have said
it was imperfect: a voice into the green world, and that world,

that beautiful, irritating, basket of details I'd have to re-present
to finish the art, to get it right, it was imperfect, yes, this too.

—Now you help me: think of them, list them,
repeat after me: everything, everything, everything, everything,

everything everything everything. Everything
every possible thing, and the desire to know each, too,

to touch, to marry the details of the world,
that space of whether God exists—which, to know,

would have all else vibrate in response: if *yes*, then
what a form, if *no*, then that too, so to know and to not know

both at once means to name everything. Everything. Everything,
and the delicacy of our approach, not to alter, to present

without holding, form, colors, shape, invention, dissolution, music.
Everything. Let's close our eyes and I'll start naming.

# Acknowledgments

_____

Grateful acknowledgments is made to the editors of the following publications in which some of these first poems appeared, occasionally in different versions or under an alternative title:

_America Magazine_: "Death Visits the Garden"

_Born Magazine_: "Among the Gospel Trees the Only Moving Thing"

_Cagibi_: "You should Put a Donkey in your Poem"

_CDC Poetry Project:_ "Facts"

_Connotation Press_: "The Space of Whether God Exists," "Japonica Rationalizes the Possibility of a Heaven"

_Image_: "Seven Words," "When the Dove Flew Overhead"

_In Posse Review:_ "The Sin Sonnets"

_Kenyon Review:_ "The Fox" "The Perennials"

_The Laurel Review_: "The Space of Whether God Exists" (section III of book in its entirety)

_Midway Journal_: "The Letting Go"

_Narrative_: "An Incomplete Encyclopedia of Happiness and Unhappiness"

_Nat.Brut, The Quarterly of New Art & Writing_: "Rabbit and Hawk"

_Pebble Lake Review_: "Invocation," "Absolution"

_Ploughshares_: "Making Small Talk, the Cashier at the Grocery Inadvertently Creates a Religion," "The Cat"

_Unsplendid:_ "The Great Disappointment"

Special thanks to my editor, Gabriel Fried.